In Quiet Realm

Published by:

Write-On Publishing

Write-On Publishing
59 Tom Brown Boulevard
Santareme, St Francis Bay. 6312
Tel: +27(0)422941023
frank@writeonpublishing.co.za
www.writeonpublishing.co.za

Edited By Frank Nunan
Book Design & Layout: Frank Nunan
Cover by: Günther Simmermacher

ISBN: 978-0-6399359-5-9

Poems by
Lawrence Mduduzi Ndlovu

In
Quiet
Realm

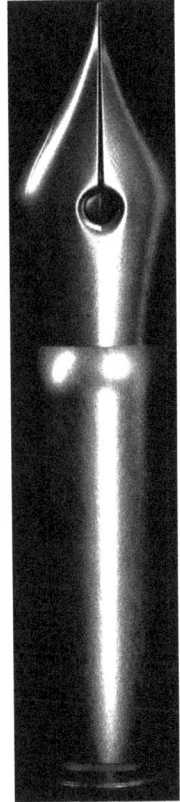

With Preface by Ambassador Lindiwe Mabuza
and Foreword by Jessye Norman

Contents

To all the people who have made me,
especially my grandparents, whom I love
and miss immensely.

Stephen Majuba Ndlovu

Zodwa Ndlovu

Samson Nkosi

Thokozile Gama Nkosi

Preface

The Quiet Realm - The Maze of Fr Lawrence's Journeys

Ambassador Lindiwe Mabuza

In this elegant, compact and complex poetry book, Father Lawrence tenderly yet determinedly escorts us through a fantastic maze of his journeys - spiritual, political and social. The very title suggests some solemn region of the soul where intangible, imperceptible but manifest grace resides. Simultaneously, we are privy to the history of his heart and his relationship with God. Hence those moments when we are drawn into a mystical world, an awesome labyrinth of being as the poet draws on his vast knowledge of Philosophy and Theology, disciplines prevalent in the poetry.

Here is a world peopled by martyrs and Saints who are Africans of all ages who, fearlessly and tirelessly, worked for rights and the good of their own people for principles and values, noble and sublime. Simply stated, the poet celebrates those virtues that elevate the human spirit.

Besides being aligned to the Divine, most Saints have the power and efficacy to qualitatively change circumstance and conditions in our lives. In the poem *"GIANTS BOW OUT"*, our Ancestors or great leaders " reside in the great balcony of heroes/toasting and singing" like heavenly choirs, not unlike Saints in Paradise "urging and spiriting" their descendants to ever- greater triumph or glory. After death, "...they stand at a distance/like matriarch and patriarch sparrows to their little ones".

7

Communication between the Giants and the living is lovingly dynamic as "when whispering the much needed solution" to their youth.

In Africa, the concept of life- after- death does not originate with Christianity, Judaism or Islam but is germane to and, integral to Africa's belief system, her Theology. That is why in his ground breaking book, ***AFRICAN RELIGION***, John Mbiti can boldly assert that "Africans are notoriously religious."

Because this special poetry book is also a Song of Wisdom, it isn't an easy read at all, with multifaceted levels and depth of meaning. Pope Francis says of Wisdom "It is the grace to see everything through God's eyes. Thus we are not alarmed when in ***NIGHT PRAYER*** the poet expresses his absolute, yes total surrender to God. All he has and does " is a gift from God". Priests live breathe and abide by what St Paul says to the Ephesians (2:8-9): "For it is by grace you have been saved, through Faith - and this is not from yourself, it is the Gift of God - not by works, so that no one can boast." (We have to assume that Father Lawrence articulates the depth of his gratitude on behalf of all good priests!)

There will be unexpected turns and surprising encounters in these prayerful verses as in "FREEDOM/ My God thy Freedom!" Flippantly or casually we think we know what "Freedom" means. But in this poem Father Lawrence flips things around as he stands in awe at the Creator's depth of gratuitous love for his creation by giving us the free will or freedom to be wise or foolish "To choose the Creator / or the other it knows not."

When I suggested to Father Lawrence that parts of the section on VIRTUES reminded me of Saint Augustine's precious book - ***CONFESSIONS*** - his response was: "Perhaps the poem GRACE. But I am more influenced by St Thomas Aquinas, even by Aristotle!" Knowing absolutely nothing about either of these great minds, I rested my case right there. What I should have remembered to ask regarding Aristotle though is "Father have you read the book by a Nigerian Jesuit priest "*THE AFRICAN ORIGINS OF GREEK PHILOSOPHY?*"

That highly researched book explains how all the disciplines the West claims to have come from Greece actually have their origins in the ancient Egyptian Temples, Universities, where many Greeks including Plato and Aristotle acquired their Philosophy. But from that brief exchange we can conclude that it is in this section pre-eminently where the Philosophy Theologian shines through.

But my curiosity pushed me to probe further into the Aristotle - St Thomas Aquinas connection. The book *SAINT COMPANIONS* (for each day) sorted me out. St Thomas Aquinas, this "Angelic Doctor" and "Prince of Catholic Theologians" was the principal exponent of scholastic philosophy which interpreted Aristotle's system in the light of Christian teaching.

In his unrivalled *SUMMA THEOLOGICA* - a summary of Christian Philosophy and Theology, (one of 60 works he wrote by the time of his death at 49) St Thomas Aquinas wrote " Since the principal aim of this sacred science is to impart knowledge of God - not only as he is in himself, but also as the beginning and end of everything especially of the rational creature." Quite extraordinary for me was the discovery that he is the composer of the Corpus Christi mass with two of our all-time Latin favourites, *Tantum Ergo* and *O Salutaris Hostia*!

VIRTUES! This beautiful, delicate section - a Song of Praise, (if you will), is compact with profound lessons for living. The didactic and touching poem BE GRATEFUL declares that we should always have a positive disposition towards life because we are all God's planned existence. In every human endeavour, as we go through various vicissitudes of life, there is always something worth celebrating since it all comes from "the unending cosmic creation". Do not submit to misery, admonishes this supremely gifted and knowledgeable musician! Why? Because:

"Surrendering to misery is foolishness
For misery   is but a dreary movement
In an altogether joyful orchestra of life."

Again we encounter the poet's marriage of Philosophy, Theology and life experience when he sums up the meaning of illness in these lines:

"For ailment though unwelcome
Can be an invitation to venerate
The hallowed temple that is your body"

We can conclude that the body has to be "hallowed" because the book of Genesis pronounces that God created humans "in his own image" which means the Blessed Trinity resides in us. What an awesome notion, a blessing!

Ultimately gratitude, even the very act of being grateful, ought to mean our surrender

"To the unfathomable greatness
Which precedes even our finest virtues."

When poetry leads to prayer one has truly entered the house of Benediction!

Though I managed to do decently in Philosophy 101 under Oblate priests, as I earlier indicated there are some complex poems here. Yet I like Father Lawrence's Augustinian GRACE: Oh Grace! At the onset, the poem proceeds from "The Dark Night of the Soul" with violence and pain when we mortals seem totally oblivious of the "Center", the "Core", the "Holy Seat" even though these are within us, eternally in our midst.

Unless we understand that Wisdom and Reason are themselves created by the "Maker" we will foolishly act like an unruly child throwing tantrums all over the place. Only by surrendering our futile search for God in wrong places and get heated or inspired from within can we get the confidence and inner strength "to unleash heavenly choruses", which is the grace to bring us to where the Omnipresent God is to be found:

>Here
>Before
>Beneath
>Between
>Within

Slavery

Moving away from a bird's eye view of VIRTUES to political poems like JESSYE NORMAN, SOUTH AFRICAN NATIVE CORP: SS MENDI; TAMBO and THE AFRICANS could be seen as either an uncanny or unlikely dive or some stupendous soar, depending on one's political perspective. Perhaps both, for in the author's footnote to the poem BEAUTY: A Recital, Father Lawrence writes: "I find that musicians with a story to tell tend to offer more than just melody, they bring to every performance every joy, pains and persons that have led to that particular moment."

The above was stated after the poet and the sophisticated London Classical Music audience at the most prestigious venue, The Royal Opera House, had been mesmerised by a superb rendition of Classics in a programme by a young artist from Alexandra Township, a "slum" area of "the wretched of the earth", as Frantz Fannon would have described those of our people colonised by Apartheid living there.

So it is indeed with Jessye Norman, the poem and personality. Since Literature is a document of history, the poem is not merely an encounter with one of the world's most renowned dramatic sopranos, mostly associated with the repertoire of German composer Wilhelm Richard Wagner. Here the nitty-gritty of slavery is stripped bare leaving us with a beautiful poem, a skeletal structure from agonising pain straight out of the house of horror. We have to reflect and bring to sharp focus the fullest implications of this most anti-African brutal crime ever visited on the peoples of Africa by European men.

Let's begin with the untold fear for both the captured, chained and scared stiff captives as well the nerve wracking flight of the escapees running helter-skelter to unknown destinations! We read in many western books of Africans selling Africans! What scandalous moral depravity! Isn't it the case of adding insult to injury calling that grossly inequivalent exchange, a sale.... the commercial transaction of a whole human being with a bottle of rum or cheap trinkets (junk)? The introduction of an addictive drink was the beginning of the destruction of African food culture.

These grotesque habits consciously perpetrated for well over 300 years visited upon at least 40 million Africans must have deformed and corroded European consciences and sensibilities (especially the DNA), to the extent that to this day we still have to deal with the psychologically abnormal consequences of racism, notwithstanding the brave Abolitionist Movement struggles of those centuries ago.

The rape of the land started with Slavery. But so did the rape of African women by men whose wives or girlfriends were in Europe or the Americas. This was the beginning of the category called "Coloured". No African woman ever denied its ethnic name to her baby. Europe normalised rape, then called the offspring "COLOURED!" On Goree Island (Senegal), enslaved African women were conveniently kept on the floor directly below where the lecherous "superior" white slave managers slept, for quick, easy access.

Slavery tried to psychologically castrate, emasculate and reduce African men into studs because, after all, we were not human, only chattels, horses. There was the large-scale disruption of normal livelihoods as well as disintegration of known patterns, customs and norms in societies where peoples' frame of reference was shattered. Mores, beliefs and intelligible societal coherent systems passed down from generation to generation were totally turned upside down, compromised, if not totally destroyed.

Then enters JESSYE NORMAN, the poem:
"Like animals
They were steered
Into vessels of indignity."

Having already been traumatised to the tenth degree and dehumanised by enslavement we are faced with compounded terror of "The Middle Passage" as described by the great Pan Africanist, W E B Du Bois in his authoritative book on Slavery "*SOULS OF BLACK FOLKS*". The more slaves loaded on each ship the better as there was safety in numbers. "Packed like sardines" means there was no consideration for health or comfort. But it also meant that even if the sick ,the dead and those "belligerent" freedom fighters resisting being enslaved were thrown overboard, there would still be a large enough number to alive to make a handsome profit for the traders in humans.

The composer of the famous "*Amazing Grace*", John Newton, saw it all and also heard the melancholic tragic African chants as he captained the slave ships. It was the slaves' mournful fighting West African chant that gave Newton the melody for the Christian words of *Amazing Grace*. How many non-Africans could even approximate Jessye Norman' s rendition of that hymn? Inspired by her Ancestors' struggles and triumphs, this all-time favourite was and still remains part of her DNA.

In the Norman poem, the poet reminds us that even in the midst of horrendous odds like working for no pay and the lynchings and beatings, yet the African continued to assert his humanity, her human being-ness, his being fully human, through the SPIRITUALS. These are a living legacy that our African Ancestors bequeathed their descendants and the world. Denying the slave the use of his own language and giving him the Bible, the intention of the Slave Master was to turn the slave into a subservient docile creature only good for taking instruction.

The slaves in their ingenuity masterfully turned the master's intention around, finding synergy with much in the Bible that was analogous to their plight. Many revolts and escapes were effected thus. "*Deep River*" is, on one simple level, the Jordan River in Palestine where Jesus Christ was baptised. On another level there is nostalgia and loneliness for home, Africa, in which case "Deep River" is the Atlantic Ocean which the slaves crossed to the oppression of the Americas. Thirdly and more frequently applicable, the song was a coded message for the intention to escape across (the Mississippi river) to the North where there would be freedom.

So as France marks her bicentennial (200 years) celebrations of the French Revolution, Jessye Norman, this distinguished survivor of slavery, segregation, plus any and many an untold indignity visited on all black people, stood there and sang whilst towering, by force of a higher moral authority, over tens of thousands gathered for this grand event.

As a VIP guest of President Mitterrand, she stood tallest, representing all generations forcefully removed through Cape Coast in Ghana, Goree Island in Senegal some via what was the Cape of Good Hope in the South and millions who ended up in graves "with foreign names", their African identity permanently deleted from history! With the most acute sense of history on French soil; in the most treasured and revered piece of real estate in France, Revolution Square, (the heart of the French Revolution) the unparalleled Jessye Norman's voice beckons multitudes of slaves long gone, their descendants plus all oppressed still locked in battles for what the Jacobins wanted in France with the rallying clarion call of the French Revolution!

Liberty!

Equality!

Fraternity!

Exit Slavery - Enter Colonialism

Slavery took Africans from their land.
Colonialism took the land from Africans.

It is almost as if the poet does not want to leave us luxuriating in the triumphant spirit of the magnificent, magnanimous voice of the African Queen of Opera in the Diaspora! As soon as the slave ship sails off the West African coast carrying the biggest CRIME and SIN of Europe (against Africa) to the America's we are forced to ask: "What about those left behind?" The ones who ran away not to be caught, or those who were too young to be useful in doing the heavy work on cotton fields of the southern USA or in the sugar plantations of the Caribbean!

The poem "ETERNALLY OWED" suggests the answer to that question:

What a sight it was
When they held her back
from hurling herself
into the sea
She wept

Trauma is experienced by those forcefully pulled out of their familiar world and who will now slave for no pay. Trauma is also the lot of the ones who remain in Africa. The intensity of losing family members, friends and neighbours in one sweep is par with the loss of land. Internally, an unprecedented mass migration of people from especially coastal regions started as no borders existed. As for the rest, the poem says

> They still weep
> for they not only lost
> those who shared their blood
> they also lost their land

The entire poem is a lamentation for the grievous loss, heart wrenching pain, the haunting and often suicidal anxiety because you know that wherever they are taken to can't be a good place for your loved ones. How can it be good if none has ever returned? How can it be good if they had to be chained and hauled into ships against their will?

Historical evidence shows that before Slavery, Africa had advanced civilisations, (Benin, Ghana, Egypt, Mali, Maphungubwe, and Monomatapa). There is evidence as well pointing to the stagnation that beset much of Europe because of endless/countless tribal wars at the same time as Africa was thriving in various sectors of human development. Imagine people fighting a "30 years war" a "100 years war" "The war of the Roses", Napoleonic wars, the countless crusades etc. etc.

The implications for the continent to have lost well over 40 million able bodied people are dire.

With construction and development processes disrupted, stagnation in every human endeavour set in. In his book, **HOW EUROPE UNDERDEVELOPED AFRICA**, Walter Rodney gives an insightful account of the extent to which the entire Industrial Revolution was literally fuelled by profits from slavery. The accumulation of wealth from Slavery led to the rise of Capitalism as a new mode of production. In the final analysis, Capitalism's acquisitive impulse is what made Slavery redundant.

The Americans fought a Civil War over whether the North and the South could be one country under either Slavery or Capitalism. The latter won the day. Across the Atlantic,

European men, in a desperate effort to ride the tide of the new system, met in Berlin (1895) and arbitrarily chopped up and partitioned Africa, each taking what was in their country's best "National Interest". Thus the scramble for Africa was sorted out with Britain, France, Portugal, Belgium and Germany poised to exploit, to the maximum, the natural and human resources of their chosen pieces of the pie on the African continent, for the maximum benefit of Europe. The converse side of the coin would be the further backward or de-development of Africa.

So the African poet cries out with searing empathy for the African victims of the devastation brought by Europe. The damage isn't just material or physical. It drives deep into the very essence of the people... the soul! Since time immemorial every culture has devised ritual for honouring their departed members. Europeans have tombstones, cairns, flowers etc. Some Jews will prepare an elaborate banquet, set a table, then leave the prepared food for late night spirits to feast while the family is fast asleep. Africans will slaughter something and/or pour libations on graves! When land is taken, so are the graves of one's dear relatives. Why dispossess innocent spirits? We might ask! The terror of colonialism is deeply spiritual. Customs are nullified, negated or simply trampled upon:

the vagi
the ones wandering
cannot offer libations...
on the graves of those
who remained with them
......for home is no more

The penetrating poignancy and tragedy of colonialism is magnified in the absurd notion that in Africa, for Africans, "home is no more." Translated it simply means security of all kinds is no more. Firstly, the loss of family (nourishment, warmth, sharing, protection, self-fulfillment), health, housing, land because of new unintelligible laws and illegal treaties with African leadership duped into signing from positions of utter ignorance, illiteracy, and fear of the almighty white skin: clothing, (since traditional production industries were abruptly abandoned by artisans on the run! Manchester woollen cloth was introduced in tropics with nary a Winter Season to replace what European missionaries decried as "sexually suggestive". Traditional attire, most suitable for Africa, had to take a back seat! The vicious attacks on what makes a being African came from all directions!

A classic case of the aberrations or criminal excesses delivered by colonial masters is the Congo, which was the sole property of King Leopold 11 of Belgium. In **KING LEOPOLD'S SOLILOQUY**, Mark Twain harshly condemns the Belgian King's grossly abusive rule of the Congo in one of the finest and most revealing political satires of this evil period Since the country was his property, King Leopold II did as he wished to the Congolese people.

The colonised had to provide ivory for European insatiable greed. As policy, those who returned without ivory from their elephant hunting expeditions had their hands chopped off. What did it matter the age or gender? Between 1895 and 1905 when the country was taken over by the Belgian Parliament, the population of the Congo was reduced from 25 to 15 million people.

Prior to Colonialism, Africa knew no poverty, as the granaries were never empty, milk and buttermilk aplenty, all year round, nuts, vegetables including wild greens,(spinach, kale, collard), legumes, organic chicken, guinea-fowl and other wild poultry, seafood, varieties of game as well as beef and goat only on special occasions, plantain, yams, sweet potatoes! No undernourishment or malnutrition here! No unemployment where co-operative labour was engaged in organised communally - according to seasons - division of work according to gender and age.

Enter World War 1

In 1917, European TRIBALISM flared up with unprecedented fury, resulting in a war that involved not only Europeans. From South Africa the Colonial Master, Britain, recruited young African men, not to fight but to be choppers and carriers of wood around places like Delville Wood where only white South African soldiers are buried. All heavy manual work, digging trenches and whatever work considered below the dignity of the gun carrying white boys, was done by them. Even during the war, the colonial master of South Africa, Britain, applied the racist policy of separating dead black and dead white soldiers! Black soldiers could not be entrusted with the responsibility of carrying a gun in Europe out of fear of what they might possibly attempt upon their return to their racism-infested home, South Africa.

On March that year the ship carrying our young recruits was rammed through the middle by a bigger ship, *Darro*, sending 600 of our young to their early death in the freezing waters of the English Channel. Pointedly the poet asks:

"Was it war that robbed of peace?

or did a settler's snare a nation's posterity rob?"

Once again, going back to the theme discussed earlier of the relation between the living, the dead and future generations to come, at a point of terrifying death by drowning "...Ancestors stood before them in warm embrace." In relevant spots IN QUIET REALM, the poet underlines and re-asserts this theme of cyclical inter-connectedness of the spirit of the dead, the living and of generations to come.

This philosophical proposition sits comfortably with Father Lawrence's Christian ethos. "The Voice of the dying" is relayed to "the living across Africa's shores" who in turn "herald" it to "future unknown generations" who will continue to struggle and eventually "in freedom's peace sail." In a different poem, AFRICANS, the poet much more assuredly teaches that not only is the sacred embedded in the African ("Before I formed you in the womb/I knew you!"), but also the African manifests

"An awareness that living.
is a recurring prayer
a movement
between
the jiving
the living-dead
and the living-God,"

Just in case some amongst us think Father Lawrence, the poet, is the latest arrival from planet Mars, hear what an established great poet from Senegal, Birago Diop, says on this subject, a comparison that not only places Father Lawrence in the credible stable of Liberation Theology advocates but aligns him squarely within the Pan Africanist mould:

"Listen more to things
Rather than beings
Listen to the fire's voice
Listen to the voice of water
The weeping of trees in the forest
...
The dead are not beneath the ground
It is the voice of our grandfathers
...
It is the darkening shadows
It is the lightening shadows
...
It is the baby on the mother's breast
...
Listen more to things than to beings
The dead are not dead

(Only a few lines randomly selected from one of the finest poems on death)

Clearly, it cannot only be Western institutions that can alone and adequately explain all the time old mysteries of creation! Nor does the sum total of all human endeavour and experience do justice in elucidation without going back to " the beginning and end" of it all, the Master, as Father Lawrence's VIRTUES have eloquently revealed.

It is neither accidental nor coincidental that the very first book by Father Lawrence should have poems on the SS Mendi and the Man of Virtue par excellence, the incomparable Oliver Reginald Tambo, popularly known as O R, Chief and Buti (brother) to some of us. I hope the reader plus all O R's political protégés and children will understand and or forgive me. You might be chastising me for not having started this Preface with him, as the author of these poems did.

The reason is quite simple. I thought it was best to discuss him in the historical context I have tried to portray in this exposé. I would hope that placing him at the end rather than downgrading this colossal patriot from the hard-earned position he rightly occupies, Chief enables our narrative to end in a wholesome fashion, a high note!

The years 1917 and 1918 mark the Centenary of two events in the annals of South African history. As already discussed, on 27th February the worst wartime maritime disaster in UK waters occurred, sending 600 of our own to their death. Yet the same year was to have a triumphant end for our country and people, the birth of O R Tambo.

At his birth, his parents named him, KAIZANA, little Kaiser, after the German head of state fighting the member countries of the Triple Entente or Alliance of Britain, France and Russia. On Germany's side was Italy, Austria Hungary and the Ottoman Empire. What was the Tribal War about?

1. Competition over military prowess! Which Alliance is stronger in warfare?
2. Alliances had a mutual defence pact to come to the aid of an attacked member.
3. Imperialism's propensity for acquiring more colonies, our land and us.
4. Chauvinistic National identity overtook sense of International cooperativeness.

Because South Africa under Louis Botha was part of the "British Empire", the country was committed to supply troops for King George V's war gamble which sent our 600 young African men to their SS Mendi diabolic death. The fact that O R's parents would dare name their son after the German leader is a clear indication that while our youth were sacrificed on the altar of a domineering colonial power in that fatally doomed ship, on the ground and *EZILALINI*, amongst our people, our oppressors' enemy was our friend. The symbolism of Kaizana's name can't be lost. Eight months after the SS Mendi disaster the Africans in our country were still seething with anger. Almost prophetically, our own newly-born Kaiser would grow up to fight the "Apartheid crime against humanity", oppression that had its genesis in slavery and Colonial rule.

In Tambo's own homestead of Mbizana, the encroaching danger from Colonialism seemed imminent in the poem TAMBO:

"Terrible objects floated
towards this pure land
The very core shuddered
Something within coiled
sensing the impending darkness"

It soon becomes clear that those who had been seen by shepherds, (O R himself had been a shepherd minding his father's stock), those very "foreign tongues" heard by village women getting ready to go to the fields, the interlopers who had even caused the leader of liberators to summon all to battle, didn't have good intentions at all. The crude exploitation of our natural resources was accompanied by the de-humanisation of the people evident in their

livelihood stolen,

person-hood reduced

We know that these dire conditions were the reasons that made O R decide to dedicate his youth and adult life to the liberation of our people. What is apparent in the poem is that the poet is not ambiguous about O R's leadership role. He is the ELDER that generations upon generations of freedom fighters have looked up to for direction, guidance, tough nerve, intellectual stimulation, father-care and sound political education.

In Oliver Reginald Tambo, the ANC, the oppressed people of South Africa and the continent of Africa had the ultimate leader we could ever have. O R left South Africa because the ANC wanted him to rebuild the banned organisation from outside. He left South Africa carrying his suitcase. He returned carrying the entire world. Patiently, persistently unreservedly, he tirelessly worked every minute of those 30 exile years until the stroke stopped him in 1989.

Before that star-crossed moment came, this absolutely selfless, self-effacing and principled leader had explained when to our people and the world when he thought we would be sure of victory, that is, when four pillars had converged. These are:

1. The mass mobilisation of our people inside the country
2. The work of the underground operatives inside the country
3. The hammering blows of MK , the Armed Wing of ANC inside South Africa
4. The mobilisation of the International Community

Just before he was struck by the stroke, O R, more than anyone else, understood precisely how these four pillars had converged. Over Radio Freedom, he had instructed the oppressed millions to "Make Apartheid Unworkable and the country Ungovernable." The country and the world gave Apartheid no quarter.

The stroke came just as he started the process of presenting the Harare Declaration first to the Presidents of Frontline States, the Organisation of African Unity, the Non-Aligned Movement and finally, the General Assembly of the United Nations. Briefly, the Harare Declaration stated that the prosecution of our struggle had advanced to such a degree that "a conjecture of circumstances exists" for a peaceful resolution to the South African conflict. Rather than a protracted armed confrontation as a sine qua non, an imperative, negotiations were clearly on the political cards.

That is why in the poem when the youth ask President Tambo

> Do you see freedom elder?
> Oh do tell us about her

OR with his scientific mind, full of confidence as a reassuring father and a political seer, proclaimed:

> "I see the exiles return
> I see one like us ruling
> I see the land bearing our name
> I see freedom."

In the end, the Catholic poet gives us Tambo, not the superb politician, but the Anglican who had wanted to be a pastor, but then chose to work full time for the freedom of our people. I believe that for 30 years President Tambo's secret weapon was his deep Christian faith. Whoever visited the Tambo home in London would have seen written on the door post, NOMTHANDAZO (Mother or House of prayer).

By conscious choice, President Tambo went into every meeting, consultation, conference, especially confrontational sessions alive with God inside him. He remained an infatigable disciple on a sacred, yes, a divine mission. Otherwise how does a man who left the way he did, without a passport, return, three decades later, his body weak from having emptied the best of himself totally for all of us but, most important, carrying back the entire world?

At the NASREC Consultative Conference of the ANC, December 1990, as he bowed down from the Presidency of the organisation he simply said:

Indeed! Then it is both touchingly fitting and appropriate that the poem ends with the most humble, modest Oliver Reginald Tambo, not in self-congratulatory adulation as persons of lesser staff would do after such a sterling achievement. Our most beloved compassionate leader and father stands in a prayerful posture with a profound sense of gratitude as

> "He whispered
> To God
> To the land
> To all
> "Mine is accomplished"

The undisputed Father of South Africa's Democracy!

Foreword

The Light Which Guides Father Lawrence

In Father Lawrence's anthology, hear the songs of his heart, the voices of the ancestors, present, imagined, alive.

This is a homage to the spirit and soul of our birth, the glories, the dilemma and the blessings of the sun and soil of the mother country.

We are honoured and grateful to come face to face before the soaring faith that makes perseverance possible.

We shall not be moved.

Father Lawrence would have us remember to hold close in our minds and hearts all that we are, all that has made us. All that we are empowered to be.

The strength of memory guides and protects.

The green plains, the hot heat, rivers crossed in dreams, prayers and laughter, the wind of forever on our skin. Freedom.

We learn that we can have all of this - any time- because truth is on our side in thankfulness and abiding love.

Jessye Norman
June 2018

In Quiet Realm

I took a tour
    Somehow knowing it was time.
    I felt pulled
    through corridors
    where life seemed to gaze
    right back into me.

    As it took me into itself
    I saw a door,
    which I had never seen before.
    On it was chiselled
    words only understood
    away from the noise,
    they read,
"in quiet realm",

    When I approached it,
    I knew I was facing
    a chamber within my own self,
    whose key I had never bothered to find,
    for I was afraid of what was within.

    I crossed that threshold
    and saw faces staring at me.
    Some faces were known to me.

Then I saw hands gesturing,
drawing my attention,
to the many long roads
that they had traversed
when gathering the matter
that has made me.

In quiet realm,
I saw other faces
of those who through their virtues,
and through my following them,
introduced me to the world.

Then suddenly
In quiet realm,
a band of what seemed like saints
appeared before me;
Africans from every lineage,
warriors of all times,
martyrs of all the ages,
I saw them,
In quiet realm.

Then I saw with new eyes,
I heard with new ears – silence.
My body refused to move,
lest it disturbed the stillness,
I understood
because I stood under
those frescoes.

Then from within
that quiet realm,

Gratitude leaned her face near mine,
for because of so wondrous a sight,
I attempted to mutter
a thank you.
Then placing her index finger,
at the door of my lips,
She whispered;
"Not yet dear
Not yet."

She turned my entire disposition,
For behind me were all the virtues:

Freedom whose daughters
    are all the landscapes of the earth,

Perseverance
    where the will to go on is found,

Grace
    that gift freely given
    at all times
    in all places,

Friendship
    That pillar that holds up
    when the self is tired,

Hope
    that beautiful luring voice ahead
    which keeps the tired pilgrim
    on his feet,

Truth
    That honest friend

Then love,
    Towards which I could only bow
    Towards which I dared not raise my eyes
    For God is Love

In quiet Realm,
    I saw the entirety of life unfold;
    laughter
    joy
    pain.

    Then I saw tucked away
    what looked like a dark place.
    I knew upon seeing it,
    that it represents,
    the lowest point of humanity –
    the absence of good.

In Quiet realm
    I found the Creator
    Present
    And that I could comprehend,
    So great a Designer,
    albeit with a manner so limited,
    caused me to weep.

In quiet realm,
    I heard gratitude
    Say to me;
    "Now
    Yes say it,
    all the time,
    everywhere
    to everyone
    Thank you!
    Thank you!
    I thank you!"

PEOPLE

"When a new person comes into your life
like a mystery about to unfold
and you find yourself marvelling
over the frailty and splendour of every human being -
Take off your shoes!"

Tracy Radosevic

Tambo

The shepherd saw them;
One crispy crystal clear morn,
While herding his father's stock,
Leading it to graze
the bountiful green pastures,
which would someday be his.

Women heard from within the tide,
that dawn while preparing their hoes,
that wave's usual rhythm,
sang intercepted by foreign sounds.

The warrior took to his drum;
as did in times past,
when danger advanced,
instructing even the furthest villager,
to gird his might,
and defend his right.

Terrible objects floated
towards this pure land.
The very core shuddered.
Something within coiled,
sensing the impending darkness.

Their feet stepped on this land,

Draping with darkness,
concealing these free horizons.
Elements hidden in the land's belly,
gutted,
livelihood stolen,
person-hood reduced.
From under the dark curtain;
a seedling germinates,
tearing through that venomous curtain,
illuminating dispelling darkness,
gazing at the freedom to come.

Young-ins fled the pangs,
that took away the joy they knew,
Under this great all-encompassing embrace
they wailed
they waited
they rested
looking upwards they asked;
do you see freedom elder?
Oh do tell us about her.

I see the exiles return.
I see one like us ruling.
I see the land bearing our name.
I see freedom,
that mother whose smile means happiness,
whose limbs mean hard work,
whose presence means home,
I see her here.

Upon the elder's declaration,
that freedom is here,
jubilations
from beneath his shade,
ululations abound!
Running,
sprinting to meet her,
the elder seeing
the cause of his joy
freedom here
freedom forever
freedom for all
bowed profoundly
then upright
his posture
then upwards
his eyes
he whispered
to God
to the land
to all
"mine is accomplished".

Ambassador Lindiwe Mabuza

The August Meteor

Upon dense village darkness,
in carefree ordinary night-tide,
when the sun's gaiety dies,
when the moon reigns,
as the day's sweat finally dries,
and silence hovers on rural skies,
a meteor dares the king of the night,
launching across in full sight,
spreading outward for all to see,
that beauty cannot be contained.

That dusty and dull August,
on Natal's inviting valleys,
August herself would like meteor,
surprise stillness,
unleashing brightness,
bedecking shores with light,
Beyond the magnificent beauty,
of Natal's unmistakable charm.

Self-imposed rulers,
regimes claiming supremacy on appearance,
lined their power in regiments of terror,
to scare even the finest warrior to silence.

Yet the meteor,
In her breath-taking distinction,
danced undeterred,
by the moon's glaring gaze.
Tyrants in tempestuous disdain,
stood dumbfounded,
as freedom's meteoric voice,
relentlessly heralded,
through dark tyrannical days,
the cries of her homeland raised:
Amandla! Awethu!
Mayibuye! iAfrica!

One August,
on Africa's courteous horizons,
an entire regiment,
worthy of decoration,
Regal,
Solid
Gracious
stood contained,
in one incomparable pearl.

Her beauty resides not with folly,
the velocity of her intention,
cuts through stratospheres,
taking to the core,
where truth resides,
shedding her warmth,
planting with maternal care,
setting ablaze with her love,
conquering pretentiousness with her truth.

The meteor provokes
from those who encounter her
a burst of transcendent company
Those of earthly dispositions exclaim
A shooting star! Make a wish!
But a wish changes no one.
This is no ordinary meteor.
This August Meteor,
Draws all heavenward,
to her very source,
beseeching prayer,
elevating benediction:
O God from Thy Infinite Love,
We thank you,
that one ordinary August day,
a meteor came our way,
and upon seeing her,
we have never been the same.

Jessye Norman

I Shall Be Heard

L ike animals,
they were steered
into vessels of indignity,
driven into silence,
by instruments of death,
stacked like lifeless wood,
reduced to numbers
their temples throbbing,
from teeth grinding,
from tears withheld,
quivering with anger.
Silenced.

Strewn across foreign land,
with their very lives,
manuring barren land,
human carcases,
bodies spent,
lowered into graves,
marked with foreign names,
surrendered to eternal silence.

From the grave,
in grounds soaking
with decades of sweat,
creation's chorus was heard,
shoots of spring
like Easter morning,
death gave way to life.

In toiling
without rest,
without pay,
without play,
they prayed,
everyday;
"Oh, Deep River, Lord;
I want to cross over,
I need to cross over."
Those supplications,
in the belly of despair,
the South,
that canvass of segregation,
their own would in time cross over.
Although they were unheard,
their own would be heard,
although they were unpaid,
Priced stools would beneath her feet
house gazing eyes,
in awe of this instrument of life,
this instrument of God.

They couldn't hear;
those auctioneers of humans,
the unrelenting spirituals,
daises that held up,
the oppressed.
To them it was noise,
a racket that shouldn't be heard,
but heard it was,
heard it is,
in grandest earthly halls,
sung by all descendants,
of the slaves,
of the free.

They didn't know,
that from the oppressed,
those very slaves,
the bellows,
of freedom's celebration,
in revolution's square,
would beckon the multitudes;
Arise Children!
Hurling her voice,
even to history's silent slave,
and to the future's hopeful free;
Liberty!
Equality!
Fraternity!

This Fight Bears My Name

To the Mothers of the Revolution
For Winnie Madikizela Mandela

Our very self was threatened,
Subjugated, cursed with ease.
What am I am to say
when their eyes ,
stare at me with sheer grief,
at the torment,
the guile so defined?
I refuse to lead them to apologise
for home is the land
and the land bears their names.
I am this place.
I am this land.

What I am to say to their being;
derided, defiled lacking peace?
When their bodies have not slept,
For all long night they sat and wept?
I must fight!
This fight bears my name.

Valleys are still adorned
With my father's footsteps,
when he too renounced silence.
Resilient,

armed with nothing but his name,
The warrior led the cry of fearlessness.
The unimposing hill of Isandlwana,
reminiscent of my grandmother's bounty.
The face in the clouds is that of my sister,
The soil so rich, splendid and healthy
Exemplifies the very nation it holds.
I fight for I can do nothing else
My father's blood speaks,
My mother's soul weeps.
It beckons even those creeks,
as if I fight for weeks,
Barring whips,
tears as ablutions,
with my every presence I fight.
Patiently I stomach derision,
Not because of it is right or might
But because I know that bruising
Can only pre-empt triumph.
Every shot, whip, curse and pain
unites me strongly
with my suffering brethren.
When the heat of unity reaches
the maximus of toleration,
there, and only there,
Does silence end
Then truest wrath
Bellows with might;
Amandla!
This fight bears my name!

When my own self bled
From Blood River to Sharpville
From Sharpville to Soweto,
From Soweto to Boipatong,
I had to fight!
This fight bears my name.

When my mother was lesser than the house pet,
My father reduced to having children as his masters,
I had to fight!
This fight bears my name!

Convinced and unstoppable,
A period to that history was necessary.
With every fist in the air,
With no words to spare,
I am unashamedly calling to being
A new story for my people.

These are Africans

Who are these,
from whom velvet
Takes its glow,
whose depth
drenches black
the precious diamond?

These are they
whose eyes take
their sheen
from the grand Nile
and the glistening Limpopo.

These are they
who have stood
the tear-downs
of slavery,
and settler's occupation,
because even the
Baobab's bark
holds up,
stands through
torrential storms
from above,
and excessive draughts
from below.

These are they
who bedeck humanity,
rescuing it
from the uncreative;

that state from which
imagination is estranged.

Their force
Reverbs from their drum,
And their step
a dance
From which
And for which
Some being other
Some being within,
Is continually praised,
Persistently Honoured,
The God
From which
Their being
Emanates.

These are they
who ask for the road,
who pray for the journey,
whose thankfulness
a humility,
an awareness that living,
is a recurring prayer,
a movement,
between
the living,
the living-dead,
and the living God.

These are Africans!

Native Labour Corps: SS Mendi

"Be quiet and calm my countrymen, for what is taking place now is what you came here to do. We are all going to die, and that is what we came for. Brothers, we are drilling the death drill. I, a Zulu, say here and now that you are all my brothers... Xhosas, Swazis, Pondos, Basotho and all others, let us die like warriors. We are the sons of Africa. Raise your war cries my brothers, for though they made us leave our assegaais back in the kraals, our voices are left with our bodies..."

(The Reverend Isaac Wauchope Dyobha)

Waters of Wars

Commemorating the Centenary of the Sinking of the SS Mendi - 20th February 1917

Was it these Isles that dared a warrior to silence;
these tides that rose to quell the brave?
Was it war that robbed of peace?
Or did settler's snare a nation's posterity rob?

The fog still and concealing sight,
a nation's destiny it could not blight,
Rhythms of home bellowed within,
Ancestral war-cries in refrain persist.

These Isles dared to silence the warrior
They know whose spirit they dared to bend
Countrymen's force bid even tide arise,
Ocean tide reaching, dancing and clashing
Retreating as if to gather strength,
Advancing, hurling, ululating
Bantu regiments in complete might.

Warriors did death before them face,
Its stench, its definiteness their sights dared,
Yet even the heat raiding cool
Couldn't a people's heat overwhelm,
a people's spirit in gut blazed
for ancestors stood before them in embrace.

Even in death's advancing silence,
Circumstance willing a turn only to self,
Even then to each other they turned;
"Wooo mtaka baba! Woo mtaka ma!
Are you dead that you do not hear my voice?"

The living across Africa's shores retort;
We are not dead!
Nor the sound of your voice unheard,
Your voice heralded even to the future unknown,
Your lying down was rightly with glee,
Knowing your own will never chart
waters of wars unknown,
your own will in freedom's peace sail.

Giants Bow Out

When as child in state of no worry,
  napping and unalarmed,
giants toiled that their heirs,
should never encounter unarmed,
the gruesome glare
of regimes that seek to disparage them.

In the silence of the night,
Therein was found their true might.
There in the their progenies slumber,
they toiled carving a future so different
from their own past so belligerent.
They dreamt of an offspring
That would not just toil for toiling's sake
But one that would create,
One that would not just imagine
but one that would be.

When giants wave goodbye,
They turning to their young like a joyous tide,
Pouring blessings of hope upon every side,
Their manner astute,
their touch gentle.
They bid the youth arise!
Arise son!
Arise daughter!
Awaken from slumber to maturity.

They must depart,
For the torment of the night is apart.
Nigh are the flickers of dawn,
Hopelessness demolished,
fear relinquished.
Giants depart for time ascribed them has expired.
Day victoriously triumphs,
their battles with night, no more.
As they recede they stand at a distance,
like matriarch and patriarch sparrows to their little
ones,
"Soar child, the ceiling has been shuttered."
Like landlords and landladies, they gesture,
"Plough child, the land is now fertile."
Like persons for peoples, they demand,
"Give youngin, there is abundance for all."

Giants wave goodbye,
Not too far for their offspring to forget,
Nor too near for the descendants regress.
They reside in the great balcony of heroes,
Toasting and singing,
but with an eye ever beholding the emerging young,
They cheer for every victory,
often whispering the much needed solution.

Now the progenies of the young slumber,
The young will do well to learn and toil,
For when their offspring awakens,
The skies ought to be clearer,
and the fields fertile.

Our Grandparents

Take us into your strength;
that shamelessly shunned
the fearful uncertainty,
of mega metropolises,
with just a haversack,
marching into busyness,
unshaken by its size.

Have we not imparted to you
That God goes before each pilgrim?
Have we not told you about
the army of the living dead
Whose indestructible edifice
Fortifies its progeny day by day?
Have we not told you that
nothing was new about these cities?
That these glistening streets
are not paved with gold
but are drenched with our
forbearer's sweat?

School us then,
School us about the art
of preserving queenship.
Teach us about serving from a throne
whose essence is dignity,
whose kingship is survival.

Walk with us
in the paradoxical pilgrimage;
here queens are called girls
And kings are boys.

That dear child
Is the crown of our existence,
The jewel of our comfort,
Knowing that our person-hood,
could not be dictated to us,
by those who lacked it most.
The cause of our joy,
is the laughter of our children,
their assimilation of our virtues,
that all people are dignified,
that they can do anything,
they can be anything.
That no amount of pain
Could ever surpass,
the happiness that comes,
with the experience
of the thriving of your own.

The beauty of life
Is to be able to come to your own,
and find in them
all that you are.

All that you are
Is a visible beam,
of the depth of love,
the might of truth,
and the splendour of grace,
which the throngs,
in your lineage built,
long before you were imagined.
Yours is to build on,
adding pedestals,
from which the future will stand secure.
Give what you have received,
give a solid foundation
for the mansions to come.

VIRTUES

*"Virtue is not the absence of vices or the avoidance of moral
dangers; virtue is a vivid and separate thing, like pain or
a particular smell. Mercy does not mean not being cruel or
sparing people revenge or punishment; it means a plain
and positive thing like the sun, which one has
either seen or not see"*

G. K. Chesterton

Gratitude

I Thank You

B eyond this vessel,
which so ably houses me,
and to my inmost passions,
it gives expression,
Beyond it,
My soul gives thanks,
for it is not to it
that I am called.

Beyond my very self,
my grand gesturing extremities,
is the truth which I serve,
though its very seat is within,
it pulls outward,
towards the fullness of praise,
towards nature's chorus,
which dances every day,
in ultimate harmony.

Even the rising sun,
tells of the Almighty's warmth,
and of relentless giving,
which knows no depletion.

The morning bird,
the early crowing cock,
are the earthly matins choir
that mimics the angelic hosts beyond

All of nature genuflects,
And I
I along with it,
In my own imperfect way
I unceasingly
Give thanks

Be Grateful

B e Grateful
  That you constitute a person,
    here,
    now,
    In this era.
    Your breath is a testament,
    of the Creator's design from all eternity.
    Your body is in itself,
    your uncompromising distinct dexterity,
    on life's grand and breath-taking tapestry.
    You are no mistake.
    Someone willed your being here,
    yes here,
    now,
    at this time.
  Be Grateful

  Be Grateful
    For moments of laughter and recreation;
    For although living demands seriousness,
    And loss often results in sadness,
    Surrendering to misery is foolishness,
    For misery is but a dreary movement,
    in an altogether joyful orchestra of life.

Be Grateful for the dignity of labour;
>for although the vineyard stands vast,
>not all workers can till its soil,
>for although the labourer yearns for rest,
>idling is a curse to an able body.

Be Grateful
>For those who behold you as mother;
>Though not all come from your loins,
>every birth means a sharing,
>in the unending cosmic creation,
>which began when the Creator,
>breathed life into nothingness,
>harkening into existence,
>the bountiful display
>of nature's simple complexity.

Be Grateful.

Be Grateful
>For times when infirmity slowed your stride;
>For ailment, though unwelcome,
>Can be an invitation to venerate
>the hallowed temple that is your body.
>Be grateful for the instrument that is your body,
>through it your allotted purpose can be realised.
>When it aches,
>soothe it.
>When it tires,
>rest it.
>When it has seen you through
>life's ever-bending meanders,
>and unrelenting hail storms,
>Reward it.

Be Grateful
> Even for the very opportunity of gratitude;
> for gratitude means to surrender
> one's self,
> successes,
> possessions,
> failures,
> hopes,
> strengths,
> fears,
> and even one's happiness,
> to the unfathomable greatness
> which precedes even our finest virtues.
Be Grateful

Freedom

My God Thy Freedom

B efore reality lays claim to produce
  In the designer's mind it is born
  Every yarn is woven
  to suit the makers mind
  It is enslaved
  to its maker's artistry eternally
  it desires nothing for itself
  so its maker crafts
  so it shall be
  But my God the glory your freedom
  To fashion with the greatest care
  kneading finest elements of rarity
  moulding your very signature onto them
  endowing them with freedom
  immense is your freedom
  it flows from the depths of your love
  For it could only be love
  that can create
  granting the creature freedom
  the unfettered will to choose
  to choose its Creator
  or the other it knows not.

Perserverance

No Regrets

Yet even now,
With knowing
gloomiest holes,
crippling helplessness,
would I still
that path take,
for although winding,
unrelenting,
lonely,
and wanting it was,
I learnt to trust
the voices in my head
and senses in my being.

Its ruthless ascent;
each step a choice,
to give in,
or to proceed,
Never
Never
Never could I give in,
Spurred on,
by impending resting,
of so glorious a descent,
and sun's roasting rays,
now behind,

and shadows now longer.
Stories over the peak,
of the mountain
an elder's expedition,
are for toddlers on elder's knee,
and for the amusement
of the young.

Foolhardy today,
ancient choices seem,
but a person they made,
And regrets?
a haven for those
shackled to history,
for voices
beyond the summit,
couldn't have whispered
differently,
or be heard
differently.
Their murmur
a rhythm
of life's cheers and warnings;
Keep going
Take it easy
Change direction
Stop
Listen
Get up
Live

Grace

Oh Grace

Rebellion pulls away,
shuddering sheepishly
away
from the Centre.
Immense
Vast
Is the Core
and mortal mind
forsakes attempts
of comprehending
that Holy Seat.
Reason
even wisdom herself,
is infant,
before its Maker.
The child rebellion,
in tantrums,
pulls asunder,
only to collapse
in the apophatic surrender.

In unknowing,
in surrender,
Yes in it,
Therein,
the tug of strength,
amid restlessness,

stands
between heart
and mind
to unleash
heavenly choruses
who announce,
the path
once lost,
is found
is found
within.

Oh grace!
Pacers,
citizens
like ant's colony,
search beyond
their bountiful,
courtyard,
yet those inclined
to you,
Oh perfect gift,
you
oh bountiful giver
are recipients,
of your ever-presence,
here
Before
Beneath
Between
Within.

Love

Love Song

My own heart
has betrayed me
   when it slowly
   gently
   bent towards the other

My own mind
rebuked it
painstakingly
teasing out
the obvious impracticalities

For a moment
I felt it oblige
and to itself
it silently returned

Then
as if to go behind my back
No
as if to go into my deepest self
where the mind cannot reach
it started to sing.

How did you feel,
when those eyes looked at you?
Pray tell what you thought,

When even your minds met?
Did you not weep for their pain?
Did you not give for their gain?

I heard it sing of love
whose melody
invaded me
and caused even my mind
to surrender to its beauty.
How could this have happened?
Could I
against my own judgement
be in love?

The Sound of Love

Then she started humming
Amidst hurried times
Between voices mattering.
Then restlessness
as if perturbed by unknowing,
for sounds so unfamiliar,
chanted at heart's ajar door,
Peeping in
Illuminating tender love,
Into that hardened muscle.

Then softer he became,
for love
that welcome guest,
rested in him.
And full,
complete he felt,
for yesterday's humming,
which crooned outside him,
is today's harmony,
that lives in him.

Friendship

Friendship's Deepest Gains

My sure and uncompromising recourse,
whose solid frontier has been my refuge.
In stumble and falls inclination,
your sure security denied my demise.

Oh truthful, solid and kind gaze,
my own insecurities are replaced,
by the steadiest certainty.
In the absence of your judgement,
the fullness of freedom and comfort,
unfolds in your joyful presence.

Safety of the mind's wonderings;
the first to whom my fads finds home.
My whims seem not to wear you out,
your deep personhood tolerates
even my most insignificant ponderings.

Of friendship's deepest gains
Is truthfulness without reservation,
Is affection with filial sincerity,
Is being in complete forgetfulness,
Shunning pernicious perilous pretences;
The everyday demanding theatrics,
Where truth can often be silenced,
To be replaced by the grins of survival.

HOPE

Hope's Gaze

L eaning on rocks,
fortresses on township bends ,
another day before them ends,
nothingness that typified yesterday,
persists even today.

That youthful steady frame,
renounces another slumber-filled day,
but it is doomed for another day without labour,
yet it rises because in its condition,
it must work for its own dignity.

Their eyes are of hope's watchful gaze;
that maybe this bright morning,
will dispel yesteryear's idleness,
and win for new pathways,
dispelling defeating stagnancy.

See them for the future they really are,
not hooligans on the side of the road,
rather dreamers on the margins
of their deep potential,
so near their abundance is to them,
yet the geographies of their birth,
the colour if of their skin
has marked them already for doom.

What is it to be young,
if it is not to dream dreams?
What is it to be strong,
if it not to be given space to build?
What is it to be born,
if life's purpose cannot be fulfilled?

Author's Note: I was in Soweto one morning when I saw a group of very young leaning on a rock at the corner of a street. I was saddened by that sight. They were not in school. They were unemployed. What a horrible way to spend one's youth.

Beauty

The Recital

He stood there exposed,
vulnerable as eyes studied him.
He stood there complete.
Standing before us,
was the whole Alexandra.
In that single gaze,
his mother we knew,
his father we saw,
they stood there.

When sounds poured out of him;
what the eye saw,
and what the ear heard,
seemed not to agree.
That small unimposing frame,
confident yet fragile,
could be heard and felt,
announcing the arrival of greatness.

He took us into himself,
captivated we were,
afraid to bet an eyelid,
Fearing that maybe we might disturb him.
As he sang,
we were transformed.

Tell us about Alexandra I heard them ask;
its edifice rough and unrefined,
its only sophistication is its chaos,
every stranger is lost there,
sounds invade every space.

His sound was Alexandra,
every layer of reality he invaded,
internal commotion he caused,
like the throngs that fill Pan Africa.

He stood there,
every stranger was lost in his voice,
the whole Alexandra stood there,
Stood there.

Author's Note: I had the great good fortune of attending the final recital of a friend at the Royal College of Music. I was also fortunate to see him at the Royal Opera House. I was moved deeply by the sight of the young boy from the ghetto called Alexandra in South Africa.
I find that musicians with a story tend to offer more than just melody, they bring to every performance every joy, pain and persons that have led to that particular moment.

Morning

All that is
awakes this morning.
Yesterday's paths
are arrested in history.
To retrace them might yield similarity,
But similarity is not sameness.
Beyond yesterday
is today's hopes and aspirations.

As far as history is from this morning,
the future too lies beyond what the eye sees.
Morning stands asking to be noticed;
begging not to be shared with the past,
wrestling off the anxieties of the future,
standing present pleading to be embraced.
The now awakens all to the perfect reality,
that this morning is the only certainty there is.

The fresh awakening breeze;
beyond the door of home's warmth,
that early blow on the still sluggish body,
shocking even the most prepared,
is but morning's consistent invitational,
to the knowledge that walking ever alone,
the renunciation of companionship,
has often left many cold and helpless.

Beyond yesterday's night
is today's morning.
This very morning is the only certainty there is.

Truth

Though piercing its gaze,
seeing through the heart's inner chamber,
should be accepted.
Though ripping bare,
Exposing deep-seated insecurities,
Should be celebrated.
Though lacking gentleness,
Rattling in its brutality,
should be embraced.
It requests no affirmation,
It stands unfortified,
It needs nothing,
It is what it is – TRUTH

LIFE HAPPENS

*"Life is what happens
while you are busy making other plans"*
- Allen Saunders

Eternally Owed

She couldn't be consoled
   when she thought of him.
   She couldn't be restrained
   when sorrow ripped her bare.
   The great sea was for her
   too great to be entered into.
   Just as ships rode the waves
   as they approached shore,
   they floated away with him,
   drifting into the unknown.

What a sight it was
when they held her back,
from hurling herself
Into the sea.
She wept
Wept for her father.
She wept for women.
She cried for her friends,
who were taken.
She waited
watched
as ships returned,
and every night,
she returned home disappointed.
Every day,
she stood on the shore,
hoping,
waiting for her father's return

She roams the streets,
now a mere vagus,
filling the roads,
laden with her belongs,
belonging no where
She has lost
her land as well.

The vagi,
the ones wondering,
cannot offer libations,
on the graves of those
who remained with them,
when others were taken,
for home is no more.

They still weep
just to see
the graves of those taken,
just to kneel,
at the place
where death descended,
just to say
to the souls of the taken:
"We have come to take you home."
They still weep,
for they not only lost
those who shared their blood.
They also lost their land.

Dark Invasion

Darkness
That dungeon in man,
an abyss from whose belly,
profanities whisper.
Often heard those voices,
when from goodness detouring,
to stroll near hell,
vile venomous vomit,
disgorges from darkness,
to dirty innocence,
and live beyond its hole.

Man has been seen,
in our life time,
Stopping,
Stooping,
to hear those voices,
to see dark's face,
only to arise,
without peace,
without innocence.
Those voices
no longer live apart from him,
they are him.

Refugees,
victims of the absence of peace,
longing for peace,
having known terror,
that reign of darkness,
flee contamination,
of their own innocence,
knocking
Knocking
knocking
at the doors of the free,
only to find,
behind what was hope's door,
despair,
no reception,
no embrace,
but instead -
the darkened one.

Author's note: I do not think we have really bothered ourselves with understanding what it means to be a refugee. It means having to abandon home and all that which makes it homely. It means being a pilgrim of hope; praying that wherever I shall seek help I shall find compassion. I do not think we have grasped fully what it means to have that hope shuttered when upon arrival no one wants to help you.

She Is With Child

My Mother's Story

Everyone in township's poverty,
invoked sacred names,
to make sacrosanct their pledges,
that no child of theirs shall know,
the indignity of oppression,
or hunger's defeating presence

Compromised was her return,
disposition sheepish and downcast,
the ordinary day's chores awaiting.
Normality's bland salutations gestured,
announcing with a whisper,
"Mama I am with child."

Paradox seemed to claim the day,
noise was stilled by silence,
complexity hushed ordinariness.
In a single glance,
love coincided with rage.
The volcano of perfect silence,
that dormant fiery mountain,
rumbled and festered within itself,
threatening with piping hot lava,
of maternal disappointment.

Refusing to succumb
to disappointment's rages,
elders' parental quiet imaginations,
yielded to the coming little man's rewards.
The joys of parenthood,
is to live to see your children's children.
As quietly as she had broken the news,
they too could be heard whispering,
To the one with child;
"Darling do rest your body
No harm must befall on the baby."

Brave should have been her name.
Of her a son was born.
He shall eat what we eat they said.
Her own aspirations forsaking,
she set out to labour for her brood.
To herself an oath she swore;
"As I grow he too shall grow
In the end, all shall be well for us."

Township Dusk

Dusk descended,
as heavy engine sounds
signalled the return of worker.

Smoke ascended,
and its layer lingered,
the child ran home,
for all the signs of day end,
had unravelled while he played.

He wore dirt on his legs,
filth concealed his true shade.
His night ablutions,
Before his slumber,
Made him itch,
As water fell upon his dry legs.

Then the home magic began;
as he settled beside the coal stove,
whose top had turned all red,
filled with the inextinguishable fire,
of the love best found at home.

Plates were brought out,
Then his grandmother,
Shared for many,
from what seemed to be a small pot,
All ate,
All were filled.

The smell of that moment,
and the laughter of home,
surpassed even the spacious outdoors,
for packed into that three roomed house,
was home with love abundant.

What of tea for three
With one tea bag?
It was really from one cup,
For inconceivable it was,
That one,
Only one,
Could drink as one,
In the presence of others.

Soweto My Everything

Children chuckle scattering about,
safe in their childish joviality,
the streets their playground,
they know how to laugh,
to escape into their special reality;
being absent to strains around them,
life pours irrepressibly from their smiles,
Soweto the only home they know.

Adjacent to laughter and life brimming,
death's silent procession passes.
spent life strides accompanied
by throngs who attest to the life
of a people even in death's certainty.
Songs of the world to come invade the air,
reminding all of the obvious destiny
that is found beyond the perfect chaos
of Soweto our home.

They were placed here you know,
in square shelters where five baobab trees
cannot stand in a row,
but of dignified stock they truly are.
See them sweeping away any accumulating filth,
bent over with short broom in hand,

determined to sweep away any squalor,
that might dare suggest that they are undignified.
Verandas slathered with brightest colour,
glistening like its keeper's appearance.
Miniature gardens deck each front yard,
relentlessly irrigated and pruned,
like its communally raised youth.
Children do not grow up in Soweto -
they are raised.

Style is an everyday phenomenon,
their pizzazz wins the streets,
music takes to the air,
permeating and conquering.
What some pay to see in a show,
is manifest on the streets
of Soweto;
the fighter's ring,
the dancer's stage,
the mourner's comfort.
and the dreamer's hope.

I Heard Him Die

Suddenly
This morning
It came
Rushing
To me;
I remember
Everything,
I remember
The dead body,
I remember even
The sound of
His voice,
As he wept
Into the night.
I remember!

That winter night
Someone shook our locked gates,
It wasn't the usual
sound of guns
that often thundered
into the night,
it was a man,
whose cries woke
even the sleep-loving toddler.

"There's a man shouting!
There's a man crying!"
"Be quiet"
they said,

"Be still"
they chided,
"These are dangerous times"
I heard them say.
Thugs too are fond
Of the concealing character
of a cold and hostile night,
the story of a township night,
and the violence of
our times
carried one huge lesson;
You hear some gunshots
Turn off your lights
Sit still
Deadly still.

That frightful night
His cries were harrowing,
All night long,
He cried for help,
All freezing night,
We wouldn't open
our doors,
we in our beds
were frozen
by our own fear.

He wept,
He shouted
Until the pitch
of his voice
lost its steady sound.

As each minute past,
His voice became
Lower,
and lower,
and lower,
until…
silence...

That winter morning
His young naked body
On Jabulani Lane
Lay dead.

It was not that he had fallen
Into the hands of robbers,
Who took everything from him,
Leaving him naked,
It was the elements of winter,
That invaded his warmth,
And as his cries lowered,
his heat lowered,
Until the cold silence of death,
Took the heat of his life away.

Guilt visited my people that morning,
When their eyes fell
upon the now silent night-screamer.
Omission was their sin;
what they failed to do
was to open their doors...

The real cold night
is when humanity
behaves against
its very own condition;
when it has to silence
from within itself
the cries of the other
that calls to it for help.
I know not the moment
When fear entered humanity;
That even reaching out
has become a sacrifice.

His own returned reverently
on the day
of his interment,
with his body
now robed with dignity,
to the place
where their own
breathed last.
I heard them say
to his soul;
"Come with us.
Come home.
Come to those who even
in death's dark night
would heed your cries."
They called him by name.
At last he found a door
That wasn't afraid to open.

I heard you die that night,
that cold dark night.
I saw you dead that morning,
that frosty frightful morning.
and although a child I was,
I knew with certainty,
that humanity
was never created to fear,
nor be complacent
at the sound of suffering.

TO GOD

When I look at the heavens, the work of your fingers,
The moon and stars which you established;
What is man that you should keep him in mind,
Mortal man that You should care for him?

Psalm 8

Night Prayer

As dark descends,
Oh dear Lord,
Guard my soul,
From all that is
devoid of light.
Into your hands
I offer myself
I offer my life
I offer my love.
All that I have been
All that I am
All that I do
Is for your glory.
Forgive those moments
When I strayed from you
Grant me the grace
And the opportunity
To do better.
If this is day my last
In this life
May I die
In your love
I am yours

You And I

Upon our path,
amidst my internal tumult,
   at times to my side I would look,
   and there You Gentle Guide would be.
   My steps you steadied.
   In steadying my frame,
   and in making my way straight,
   you silenced the storm in me,
   and in me found a home.

   Often lonely it felt,
   not even a passer-by
   to stop and quiz,
   about the journey's challenge.
   You found me,
   and to my side your tug,
   meant not solitary my walk,
   you were with me every step.

   I often felt us soaring
   on carriages of Your spirit,
   And suddenly it all seemed alright again,
   and at a far glance
   it seemed not to affect me,
   You had taken me out of the abyss,
   and won me for your heights,
   Beyond the hardships that whispered inability.

Walk with me again dear Saviour.
Rest forever in me Prince of peace.
Walk with me always faithful guide.
For I shudder at the thought of your absence,
And without your grip I am rendered weak.
Without your assurances all is bleak

To My Voice O Lord

To my voice
O Dear Lord
Incline your ear
Hear my cries
Let my voice
Be not to your ear
the rambling of
of an appreciative child

To my cries Lord
O Dear Comforter
Lend your relief
See my tears
And be moved
To show mercy

I plead o Divine Master
That when to thee I come
Close not your door
In front of me
Your servant
For only you
Are my recourse
Only you
Are my all

Lord That I May

May my eyes see
the splendour of your creation.

May my ears hear
your saving Word.
May my voice
unto thee sing
my word be only of your love.

May my arms stretch
to embrace the stranger,
and to offer praise.
May my legs walk
the fields of your great bounty.

Lord that I may see,
that I may hear,
that I may sing,
that I may do,
that I may be yours

IN THE END

"I open my mouth to the Lord,
And I won't turn back.
I will go!
I shall go!
To see what the end's going to be."

Negro Spiritual

Beyond

May I within death see,
and for myself confirm,
  that silent countenance,
  and perfect peace,
  is true even from within it.

May I the other side
of hard work see,
  the reward of goodness,
  the diadem of forgiveness,
  which for me amidst many choices,
  meant the pathway to happiness.

No may I beyond death see,
and for myself confirm,
  that beyond it,
  is found the fullness of peace,
  and its transitory silence,
  lays down my path,
  for loud wordlessness,
  fulfilled longing,
  and the end to so many beginnings.

In the End

I shall recline upon a rocking chair,
needing no entertainment,
for all the time,
my life will play itself out.
Splendid it shall be,
for finally this project,
when beheld in totality,
will mean - gift.

I shall marvel at the times
when the weight of my life,
Hung on a thin thread,
and thoughts of its snapping,
meant my own demise.
I shall giggle,
when I remember my sobbing,
and hallucinations,
that often convinced me,
that I had already succumbed,
that there was no thread.

I leant to trust that day
that nothingness,
is meaningless,
for threads exist,
on which hope hangs,
from this reality,
and the strength to come.

I shall recall my childish ways,
tantrums out of my own wanting,
as mere bursts of unused energy,
before meeting that true balm,
patience which soothes tempestuousness.

I shall caress my shoulders,
at the thought of love,
for even reason,
is arrested by so great a guest,
something divine happened,
I was lost into the other,
selflessness became the greatest gift
I could give myself.

For unto grace I shall sing,
for carried was I,
in moments when I looked down,
to see the feet suspended,
yet I still seemed to be standing,
for grace had counted each step,
before any stride was made,
and below my chin,
tilted heavenward my head,
when all seemed to pull down.

Early Night

To my dear friends who died too young

Youth slumbered,
with bountiful temerity,
and at that demise,
life's quality,
stood questioned:
What of living today sparingly,
as if tomorrow's bounty stands guaranteed?
What of words reserved today,
only to be eternally unsaid?

Youth slumbered,
and its demise,
dealt a harrowing reminder,
to the living,
an awakening to the now.

This death is no silent invitation;
but a loud awakening,
to live
without holding anything back.
To laugh
until the voice is suspended
and surety of breath is questioned.
To smile
as if to embarrass the sun
rendering it incompetent.

To sing
until the angelic hosts
are silenced in awe.
To love
until love is deemed staple.
To cry
to the point of sleep.
To hold
until grip means security.

Defying Death

For a moment
   Death's dreadful entry,
   dimmed our joy,
   and from us
   your laughter seemed silent,
   and between us
   it seemed a village had vanished.

Death risked to take unto itself,
the mantle of finality.
Death has had to learn,
that although the transitus,
is mediated by him,
finality belongs not to him.
In taking finality from death,
we have refused,
that all that you were,
all you are,
be silenced.

Upon the loftiest places,
and deep into obscurity,
your name shall be heard.
Upon every new signage
everything marking birth,
not death,
every new venture,
will bear your name,
In the sight of all,

On the ears of many,
and on our lips,
your name
will be spoken
and heard.

And death will in wonder,
inquire unto death's self;
how is it that your name was not consumed?
For all about life,
still speaks of you,
as fully alive.

As we speak your name,
We cast your patronage,
all your virtues,
upon whatever it is,
that holds your name as its own,
So that not only your name is heard
but also all that you are,
all you represent,
may be felt.

And unto each day,
we claim you apart from death,
setting you apart,
for creation,
and life abundant.

Eternity's Threshold

I have cherished that uncomfortable tug,
which plagued me to the point of scruples,
Continuously adjusting, turning, redoing,
seeking to quench perfection's thirst,
and never achieving contentment.

Happiness has often visited me,
often with suspicion I greeted her,
for lurking in her haversack,
was the ever-tempering sadness.

I have known of completeness,
through my very own incompleteness,
although sufficiency was frequently allotted me,
it could never my goblet fill
within and without it,
the knowledge of the existence of More,
meant the unending longing to be filled.

I now standing on eternity's threshold know,
standing closer to it life's yearning seems to subside
and perfection stands attainable,
incompleteness is made complete,
it overflows and over it runs,
and happiness holds no sudden end.

Pula

Rain

The African Blessing

May the rains descend
And chase droughts away
May the seedling of hope
Prosper in abundance
May your field's sprouting
be the flowering of your peace
May the shelter of your trees
Be the arms that stretch out
Granting protection and security
May life gain
May peace reign
May the Giver of blessings
Bless
Pula! Nala!

About the Author

Lawrence Mduduzi Ndlovu is a Soweto-born Catholic Cleric, Lecturer, writer, poet, speaker and arts enthusiast.

As a writer he has contributed to several publications through his columns in Spotlight Africa and The Daily Maverick. He has also written for The Thinker, The Huffington Post, News 24, The Southern Cross and The South African.

Lawrence read philosophy and theology at St John Vianney Seminary Pretoria, Heythrop College, University of London and the Bellarmine Institute in London.

He is a lecturer in theology department at St Augustine College of South Africa. He is Chairperson of the Choral Music Archive NPC and is a trustee of the St Augustine Education Foundation Trust and an Advisory Council Member of the Southern Cross Weekly. He was listed by the Mail and Guardian in the Top 200 Young South Africans list for 2016.

He is also the recipient of the 2016 Youth Trailblazer Award from the Gauteng Provincial Government for his outstanding contribution to youth development.

www.ingramcontent.com/pod-product-compliance
Lightning Source LLC
Chambersburg PA
CBHW061149040426
42445CB00013B/1626